D1621171

547

- 2 JAN 1987

23 DEC 1991

-5 DEC 1992

30 JAN 1987

8 JAN 93

26-02-87 .

20 APR 1995

- 3 OCT 1988

26 Oct 1988 .

0 9 MAY 1989

GARLANDS
HOSPITAL

15-89

-7 JUN 1989

29 NOV 1989

746.46

FITZRANDOLPH, M. and
FLETCHER, F.

Quilting.

## CUMBRIA COUNTY LIBRARY

This book is due for return on or before the
last date above. It may be renewed by personal
application, post or telephone, if not in demand.

C.L. 18

# QUILTING

*Traditional Methods and Design*

Mavis FitzRandolph and
Florence M. Fletcher

# Dryad Press Ltd

London

# CONTENTS

© M Fitz Randolph and F M Fletcher

Fourth edition published in 1972
This edition first published 1986

All rights reserved. No part of this publication may
be reproduced in any form or by any means, without
permission from the publisher.

ISBN 0 8521 9656 3

Printed by
Biddles Ltd, Guildford
for the publishers
Dryad Press Ltd
4 Fitzhardinge Street, London. W1H 0AH

# QUILTING

The craft which provided the medieval fighting man with a protective jacket is now used, in a thinner, lighter, version, to make practical and beautiful things for modern use and wear. The essential feature of traditional quilting is that a layer of padding is held in place between two pieces of material by running stitches which go right through the three layers and outline the pattern shapes, so that these stand up in relief, and make exactly the same design on both sides. The work is sewn by hand, in a quilting frame. This reversible quality, and the great variety of patterns which even a beginner can design, are the outstanding features of traditional quilting.

The pattern units which have been handed down in families, varied, and invented, by the traditional quilters have been drawn and printed by CoSIRA, based in Salisbury (see list on page 48). As a home industry quilting was carried on in South Wales and the north of England until about thirty years ago; now it is practised as a hobby by many people all over Great Britain, the teaching methods having been derived usually from the traditional workers.

The work is also imitated by machinery, but the mechanical precision of mass-produced quilting contrasts poorly with the rhythmic, sensitive lines of the hand-sewn work. Moreover no two hand-made quilts need ever be exactly the same, even if the same two or three pattern units are used in the design, whilst infinite variations are possible to any worker who has access to the immense store of these units. The special decorative effect, the warmth and lightness, and the individuality of each piece of work, ensure the continued popularity of traditional quilting.

There are several other kinds of quilting, known collectively as *linen quilting*, which have different techniques and are therefore not dealt with here.

# WHAT TO QUILT

Bed coverings, from full size to cot quilts, and garments such as jackets and coats of various kinds, make the most of the warmth and lightness of quilting, as well as its beauty. Cosies for the tea or coffee pot are also practical. Quilted cushion covers are popular and look effective, although the warmth of quilting and its two right sides are wasted. The full beauty of the patterns shows best in a large quilt with space for contrast of texture and line, but it is wise to begin with several small pieces of work, so that the stitches in each may be fairly uniform, and undertake a bed quilt only when technique has so improved that the last stitches will match the first.

# APPARATUS AND TOOLS

The first essential is the frame (Fig. 1) consisting of two long bars (rails) and two flat pieces (stretchers) which fit through slots in the rails and are held in place by pegs fixed in holes. Two straight-backed chairs, or trestles, are needed, on which the frame will rest steadily. Each rail has a length of braid tacked along its inner edge. A small frame, with 36 in. lengths of braid, is big enough for making cot quilts, cushion covers and garments if the material is not more than 36 in. wide. For a full-sized quilt the frame must be long enough to take the full length or full width of the quilt (generally 90 in.); this big frame can equally well be used for the small pieces of work and some quilters prefer it because its weight makes it steadier, but the small frame, needing so much less space and being easier to carry about, is often chosen by beginners.

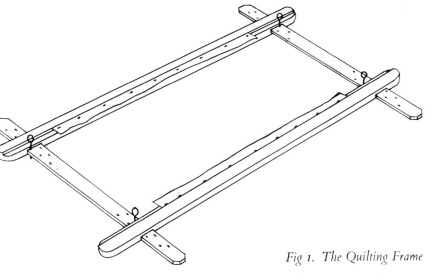

Fig 1. *The Quilting Frame*

Several dozen needles (betweens No. 9) are required, because they are used not only for sewing but also instead of pins for fastening the work; they leave no mark, even in the most delicate materials. If pins are preferred these must be the steel ones, sold as dressmakers' pins. A large yarn needle is used for marking the pattern, and also a piece of tailors' chalk.

# MATERIALS

The same material is generally used for both sides of quilted work (called the top and bottom covers) except for cushion covers, in which the underside is not seen and can therefore be a less expensive cotton or closely woven muslin. In estimating the quantity of material needed, allowance must be made for a little to be taken up by the quilting, as much as 2 in. each way in a big quilt and 1 in. on each piece of a garment. In a big quilt, or a garment, there must also be allowance for the seams, and possibly the selvedges will need to be cut off because in some materials they show through as an ugly streak down the quilt. Never have a seam down the middle of a quilt, even if, to avoid it, one length of material must be split and an extra seam made.

Material for quilting should be closely woven, soft and smooth and easy to sew through, with a slightly lustrous surface but *not* shiny. The quilted pattern is shown up in relief by the play of light and shade and if the material is too dull the pattern will not stand out clearly; if, on the other hand, the material is too glossy the high lights will give a spotty effect and spoil the pattern. It is wise to choose a washable material since home laundering is the safest method of cleaning quilted work. Silk, crepe de chine or dull satin are ideal materials; cotton poplin is very effective and it wears and washes well, but may be found rather hard to sew through. Any rayon material that is wiry in texture, or shiny, should be avoided.

The quilt should be sewn with No. 40 cotton (not mercerised cotton or "silk substitute", which are not strong enough), or *strong* silk on silk material, to match the top cover. Tacking cotton and several yards of tape are also needed.

Quilts may be padded with lambs' wool, cotton wool or wadding, domette or a blanket. Wool, the traditional padding, is not much used now except by Welsh quilters, who still prefer it for its warmth and lightness and the way in which it always fluffs up again after washing. It can be bought "clean scoured for quilting" from Welsh woollen mills, but it may need further washing, should be carded to make the staple lie straight, and must then be laid carefully on the work, piece by piece.

Cotton wool is sold in pound packets, which should be carefully opened out (the sheet measures about 48 by 45 in.). Cotton wadding (sold usually in 12-yd. lengths 36 in. wide) is on a sized backing which makes it easier to handle. The best quality of cotton wool or wadding is worth the extra cost; the medicated cotton wool sold by chemists should never be bought for quilting because it absorbs moisture. A single layer of cotton wool or wadding is generally considered enough padding for modern quilts, but two layers, put in with the "skins" together, may be used to make a thicker quilt. Even three layers were sometimes used in the past when our ancestors liked to sleep under something thick and heavy !

Domette, a manufactured woollen lining sold by the yard, ready for use, is liked by some quilters for garments because it is a very thin, light padding and yet warm. An old blanket was a popular padding for the ordinary household quilts of the past.

# DESIGNS
# AND THE MAKING OF TEMPLATES

An attractive feature of traditional quilting is that a new pattern is planned for each piece of work, and this adds interest from the worker's point of view. Although pattern planning and marking is skilled work it is not so difficult as might at first appear, because the patterns are built up with simple shapes (units) which are marked in outline from templates cut out of stiff paper or card.

The naming of quilt patterns is arbitrary. One unit may be known by different names in different districts, or even in different families in the same district. We have heard the *twist* called *cable*, *rope*, *trail*, *dog trail*, *chain*, *lost chain*, or *English chain*, and one old lady called it *plate* "because I mark it with a plate"—a rough and ready method of getting the outer scalloped line, the rest being filled in freehand. One name may also be used for two or more different patterns; in South Wales *rose* often means the *snail creep* (Fig. 15), but a North Country woman speaking of a rose generally means one of the units shown in Figs. 9, 10 and 11. We have chosen one name for each of the units illustrated in this book and have sometimes invented one; *Scotch diamonds* were taken from an old quilt made in Scotland, and *Victoria diamonds* from an eighteenth century petticoat in the Victoria and Albert Museum. There cannot be any "right" or "wrong" about the names; the variations are natural in a craft which has been handed down through centuries from one generation to another, each quilter either adopting a name she has heard or inventing a new one.

## The Drawings

*Continuous lines* indicate the template, or the outline

marked by it. *Broken lines* are those which are added in freehand drawing for sewing. In some diagrams *dotted lines* are used to show construction; these are not part of the pattern.

As there are various names for the patterns, so there are various templates for marking some of them. We have chosen those which seem to us the most satisfactory for beginners; the experienced quilter may find that a different way of marking the patterns suits her better.

TEMPLATES BASED ON A CIRCLE. Circles can be drawn with compasses or, in the traditional way, with an egg cup, glass, saucer or plate, according to size required. Figs. 5 and 6 show the simplest use of the round template, with the circles linked or overlapping. If this *ring* pattern is used as a border, rule a line as a guide and mark the overlap by small notches in the edge of the template. To use the pattern in a circle, chalk a large circle to pass through the centres of the little rings; snip out a hole in the middle of the template so that you place it each time exactly on the circle.

Figs. 7 and 8 show the *wine glass* marked on a perpendicular and on a diagonal axis, with a variety of fillings. On a small scale, without fillings, it is used in the border of the Durham quilt, Plate II.

Fig. 2 shows how to make a template for a variety of units, Figs. 3-13 and many others. Fold the circle across its

Fig. 2. *Construction of templates*

Fig. 3. *Star*

Fig. 4. *Shell*

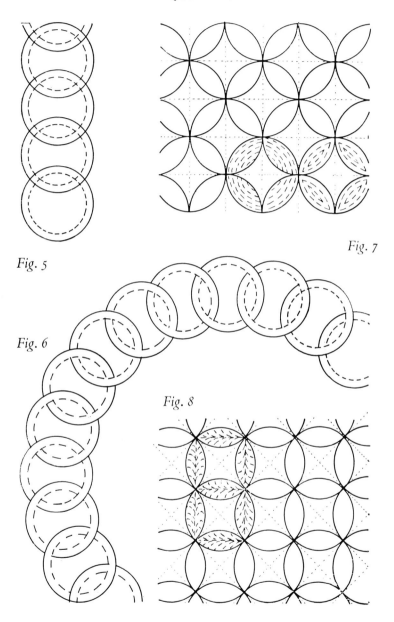

Fig. 5

Fig. 7

Fig. 6

Fig. 8

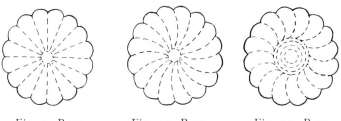

*Fig. 9. Rose*    *Fig. 10. Rose*    *Fig. 11. Rose*

centre into any number of sectors and cut for points (*star*, Fig. 3) or scallops (Figs. 4, 9, 10, 11 and 12) and for a hole in the centre. Unfold and you have your template, which becomes a *rose*, a *shell* or a *hairbrush* according to the way you fill it in. The ring in the centre is always marked,

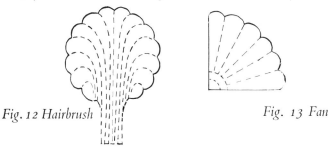

*Fig. 12 Hairbrush*    *Fig. 13 Fan*

large or small, to avoid a number of lines meeting at one point which would have a confused effect when quilted. The *hairbrush* (Fig. 12) is a *shell* (Fig. 4) with handle added. The fan (Fig. 13) is one quarter of the rose; it is a useful corner pattern which can have a great variety of

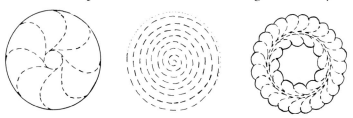

*Fig. 14. Whorl*    *Fig. 15. Snail Creep*    *Fig. 16. Feather Circle*

fillings. As a simple quadrant (without the scallops) it appears in the corners of the Welsh quilt (Plate I). The *whorl* (Fig. 14), which is seen in the *Weardale chain* (Fig. 25) is marked from an unscalloped template, and so is the *snail creep* (Fig. 15). The *feather circle* (Fig. 16) is a popular pattern in the north, used either in a large size as part of the centre pattern on a quilt (see Plate II) or smaller; for instance, for a cushion cover. In a large size it is best drawn by marking three concentric circles at equal distances apart and marking the scallops on inside and outside edges with a shilling before filling in the lobes.

BORDER PATTERNS: A template (Fig. 17) which is easily constructed from a circle by extending the sides to make an oval gives the *spectacles* (Fig. 18) and *chain* (Fig. 19).

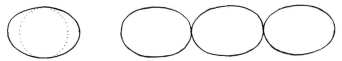

*Fig. 17. Chain template*      *Fig. 18. Spectacles*

*Fig. 19. Chain*

The *twist* (Fig. 21) is made from a similar template (Fig. 20) pointed at the ends, with notches on its edges and an oval hole cut in the centre. When marking the simple *twist*, draw only from each point to the more distant notch and round the central eye; then move the template on so that its point exactly meets the end of the eye. To work the pattern round a corner, start marking it on each border at the same distance from the corner (and of course make the

*Plate I* : A WELSH QUILT

The *fan* corners of this Welsh quilt are repeated in a slightly extended form along the border as the *sea waves* pattern. The centre is made up of four overlapping circles with *leaf* fillings in the spaces enclosed by their overlap ; a fifth circle of the same size, its centre in the middle of the quilt, divides the pieces of the four circles between the leaves ; various fillings of the spaces complete this effective pattern. Except for the *chestnut leaf* corners the other patterns are all geometrical. The straight lines of the chevron border and the small diamonds contrast well with the big curves.

*Plate II*: A QUILT MADE IN COUNTY DURHAM

The handsome centre of this Durham quilt is made up of a rose surrounded by 7 *cowslip leaves*, a *feather circle* and 12 *pairs of scissors*. The *lined twist* border is echoed by the smaller, plain *twist*.

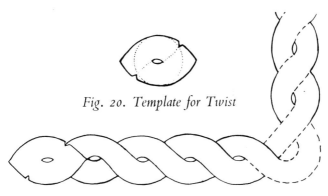

Fig. 20. Template for Twist

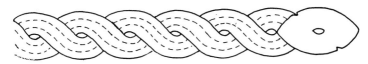

Fig. 21. Twist

template of the right size to fit into the rest of the border);
then draw in the two "ribbons" to fit the corner space.
Sometimes a *rose* is put in instead of making the twist turn
the corner (see Plate II). When the *twist* is worked in a
larger size it needs a filling and may become a *lined twist*
(Fig. 22)—notice it in the two forms, in different sizes, in

Fig. 22. Lined Twist

Plate II. To mark the *feather twist* (Fig. 23 and see Plates III
and IV) chalk the outline of the same template and mark
scallops along the edges, mark the two lines for the stem
along the centre of each feather and then complete the

Fig. 23. Feather Twist

17

filling. For the *trail* (Fig. 24) mark *all round* the same template, which is also used for the *Weardale chain* (Fig. 25) except that in this case its central hole should be a mere pinprick. First mark a series of outlines all round the

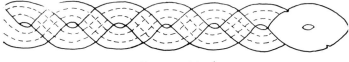

*Fig. 24. Trail*

*Fig. 25. Weardale Chain*

template, laying it point to point; then another series overlapping these, the points each time at the centre marks of the first series.

Two parallel lines ruled with chalk to mark the width of the border will be helpful in keeping these patterns from waving up and down. Any of them may also be used round a circle (see Fig. 57); draw the circle first and keep the eye of the template always on this line. The pattern will need a little adjustment, some curves being extended and others shortened.

The template for the *plait* (Figs. 26 and 27) is rather difficult to draw, but try this method, following the diagram. Draw two parallel lines to mark the width of the plait and mark two and a half scallops on each side with the middle of each exactly opposite the V on the other side, the width of each scallop being two-thirds of the width of the border. Lightly draw in all the lines of the three ribbons, keeping their width even, and they will form the triangular openings, two and a half with their points down and two

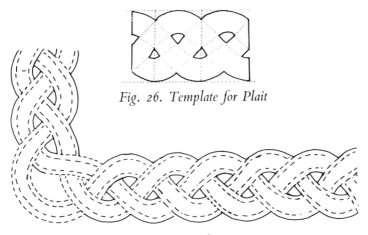

Fig. 26. Template for Plait

Fig. 27. Plait

and a half the other way up. Cut out the template with scalloped edge and the triangular holes. To turn a corner with this pattern proceed as with the *twist*.

The next series of drawings shows variations of the *hammock* pattern, the lower outline of which is a semi-circle; a shorter curve joining the tips gives the template.

Fig. 28. Hammock

Fig. 28 is the simple form, which can be elaborated into the *cord and tassel* (Fig. 29).

Fig. 29. Cord & Tassel

19

The *double hammock* (Fig. 30) template is made of a semi-circle below and two quadrants above; a little laburnum leaf pattern is added at its points.

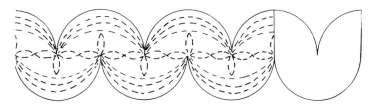

*Fig. 30. Double Hammock*

Fig. 31 shows how the *feather hammock* is elaborated from the single hammock template. The *feather wreath* (Fig. 32) may be used, either way up, as a border, or singly on a cushion and in many ways as part of a quilt design. It is marked from a double template like two *hammocks*.

*Fig. 31. Feather Hammock*

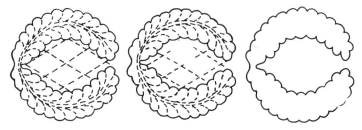

*Fig. 32. Feather Wreath*

The *running feather, straight feather* and *worm* are shown with their templates in Figs. 33, 34, 35. The *worm* can have a variety of fillings—chain, chevron and so on. The *running*

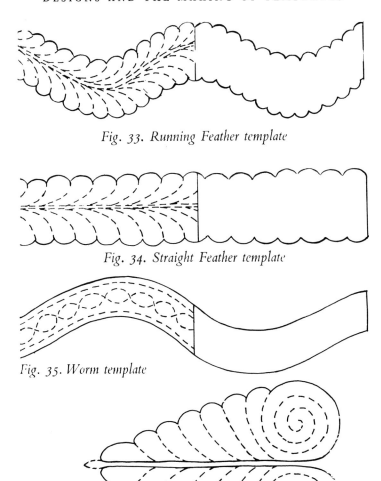

Fig. 33. Running Feather template

Fig. 34. Straight Feather template

Fig. 35. Worm template

Fig. 36. Pair of Scissors

*feather* is effective not only as a border but also in pairs running from end to end of a quilt, with or without a border, and with *diamonds*, or *diamonds* and *roses* alternately, fitted into the bulges.

MISCELLANEOUS UNITS. The *pair of scissors* (Fig. 36) is shown used in two different ways in Plate II and Fig. 59. Various feathers (Fig. 37—see also Fig. 56 and Frontispiece —Figs. 38 and 39) and the *coxcomb* (Fig. 40) are useful in

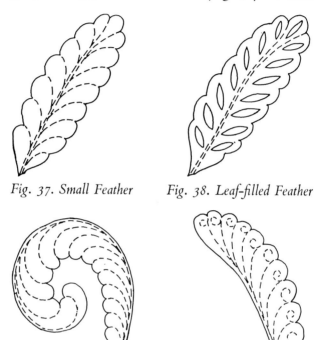

Fig. 37. Small Feather        Fig. 38. Leaf-filled Feather

Fig. 39. Curled Feather        Fig. 40. Coxcomb

building up more elaborate patterns. The *true lover's knot* (Fig. 42) looks complicated but the template is not difficult to construct. Cut out a circle and fold it in eight across the centre; mark each radius in eight equal parts as a guide for drawing the shape shown in Fig. 41, keeping the double lines the same distance apart. Cut out only the continuous lines of the diagram. Unfold the template and mark the lines for stitching, which go alternately over and under.

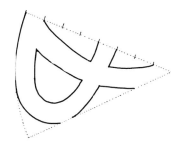

Fig. 41. *Construction of template for True Lover's Knot*

Fig. 42. *The True Lover's Knot*

23

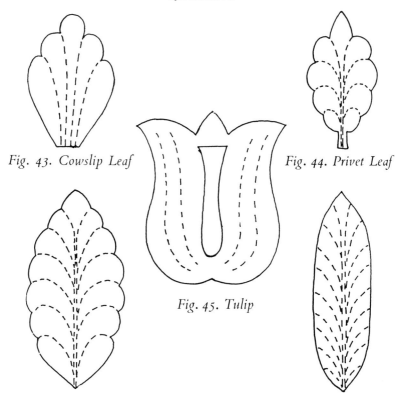

Fig. 43. Cowslip Leaf

Fig. 44. Privet Leaf

Fig. 45. Tulip

Fig. 46. Honeysuckle Leaf

Fig. 47. Elder Leaf

A few of the many *leaf* patterns which are particularly useful in designing small pieces of work are shown in Figs. 43 (*cowslip*—see also Plate II), 44 (*privet*), 46 (*honeysuckle*) and 47 (*elder*). Fig. 45 is the *tulip*, which was taken from a template used by an old quilter of Allendale, Northumberland.

The *bellows and star*, Fig. 48, was a popular old north country pattern which was also used in Dorset. In using the template for the *bellows* (shown at the bottom of the diagram) only its sides are marked; the *star* (template shown inside the *bellows* template) is an elongated form of the *rose*.

Fig. 48. Bellows & Star templates

The pattern can be varied by using different fillings and it is used singly as a border or, like the drawing, as an all-over pattern running the length of the quilt.

BACKGROUND FILLING PATTERNS. Fig. 49 shows the *square diamonds* and Fig. 50 the *lozenge-shaped diamonds*— less usual, but more elegant (see Plate III); *double diamonds* are more striking, but of course they involve twice as much

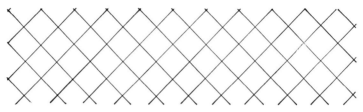

*Fig. 49. Square Diamonds*

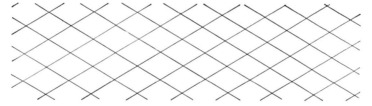

*Fig. 50. Lozenge-shaped Diamonds*

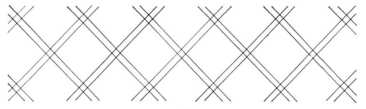

*Fig. 51. Double Diamonds*

work. *Basket* (Fig. 52) is a good background for a small quilt without a great deal of other pattern. *Scotch diamonds* (Fig. 53) is one of the prettiest backgrounds, and adds

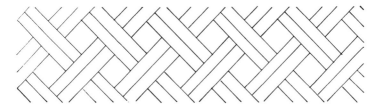

Fig. 52. Basket

Fig. 53. Scotch Diamonds

interest to any piece of work (see Frontispiece). *Victoria diamonds* (Fig. 54), like *basket*, are based on a triple diamond pattern. The middle line of the three in each direction is continuous; the others are marked only between the points at which they cross. For all straight-lined diamond patterns a flat ruler of suitable width is the best template. *Diamond chain* (Fig. 55), a good all-over pattern of a more elaborate kind, can be varied by the use of diamond fillings (see Plate III); it is made up of *chain* in two sizes arranged, as the dotted lines show, on a *diamond* foundation, from which the template can be constructed.

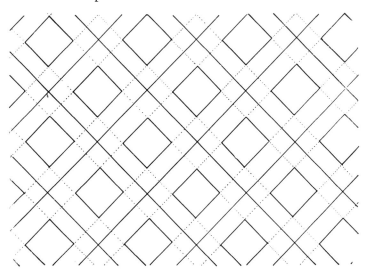

*Fig. 54. Victoria Diamonds*

*Fig. 55. Diamond Chain*

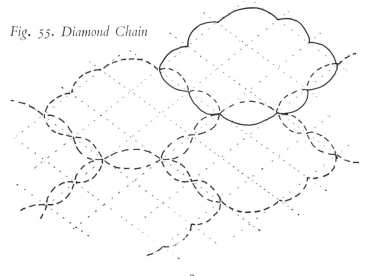

DESIGNS FOR VARIOUS PIECES OF WORK.    Fig. 56, a
suggestion for a tea cosy, and Fig. 57, for a cushion cover,
show combinations of some of the units already described.
Fig. 58 shows a new variety of *feather* as it might be used
for a cushion cover or a quilt centre. Fig. 59 shows the

*Fig. 56. Tea Cosy design*

construction of a pattern made up of *pairs of scissors* with
points inwards. To make it, cut out a circle of the size
needed and fold it into eight; make the scissors template
to fit inside this sector without touching the edges.

A different type of pattern is shown in Figs. 60 and 61,
the centre and corner of a beautiful quilt made in Northumberland about 1870; its background of very small
*diamonds* is not shown in the drawings.

29

*Fig. 57. Design for square cushion*

Fig. 58. A Centre Pattern

*Fig. 59. Pair of Scissors as a Centre Pattern*

*Plate III* : A NORTH COUNTRY COT QUILT

The patterns are *feather twist* (note how it turns the corners), *diamond chain* and *lozenge-shaped diamonds*.

*Plate IV* : A QUILTED HOUSECOAT

Note the graceful lines of the pattern on this housecoat and how the *feather twist* grows out at the bottom corners into a big curved feather.

*Fig. 60. Centre of an old Northumbrian quilt*

33

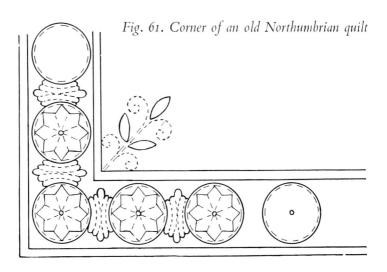

*Fig. 61. Corner of an old Northumbrian quilt*

# METHOD OF WORKING

Although every stage of the work is carefully described below, no description can take the place of lessons from an experienced quilter, especially in learning how to plan the patterns, to make and use templates, and the method of sewing.

In making a big quilt the seams must be sewn beforehand and ironed flat. Regularity and firmness of sewing is very important but judges of fine needlework consider that no machine sewing should be used on a piece of hand work; the mechanical regularity of a machined seam shows plainly on the finished quilt. Mark with a warm iron a $\frac{3}{4}$-in.turning on all edges. For a garment mark the outlines of the paper dressmaking pattern clearly on the top cover, allowing the extra inch each way for quilting. For a tea cosy, a round cushion cover, or any other piece of work that is not rectangular, mark its outline; these should not be cut out before quilting because cut pieces are liable to be pulled out of shape while being worked.

## *The Pattern*

Many quilters, particularly in Wales, set up the material in the frame and then mark the pattern gradually, as they work. We consider that marking the whole pattern on the material before the work is put into the frame is easier to learn, and therefore it is described here. The work should be designed to fill the whole space and this is usually done by means of main patterns and all-over background patterns, or "filling". Balance, contrast and clearness are all important; never forget that it is the *spaces* enclosed by the lines of sewing that will stand up and form the pattern, except where very close lines of stitching are used for contrast, such as a tightly-worked *snail creep* (Fig. 15) or *diamonds* marked with double or treble outline (Fig. 51). Remember, too, that the sewing serves the practical purpose of holding the padding in place and therefore there should be no unquilted spaces measuring more than about 2 in. across.

In planning the design consider the use to which the work will be put. A cushion cover needs a bold, simple pattern with the main interest in the centre because that is the most conspicuous part of the cushion (see Frontispiece). For a bed quilt the pattern may be designed in various ways; the most usual is a centre pattern and one or more borders, with possibly corner patterns. (See Plates I and II). The centre pattern of the quilt should fit the top of the bed. One of the longways patterns, such as *bellows and star* (Fig. 48) or *running feather* (Fig. 33), repeated to make up the necessary width, with a border, is very effective; or an all-over pattern such as *diamond chain* (Fig. 55) or *wine glass* with one of its many fillings (Figs. 4, 5). An old-fashioned method was to use strips of several different border patterns longways down the quilt.

For a cot quilt it is a mistake to try to reduce the pattern from a large quilt; it will probably be too elaborate. A design containing fewer units is generally effective (see Plate III).

Garments are perhaps the most difficult to design and need careful thought. Always remember that the garment will be worn, not spread out flat like a quilt. To avoid a top-heavy look, have the weight of the design at the bottom and let the pattern appear to grow upwards, in graceful shapes; a curved background pattern, such as *scales*, is less stiff than the angular *diamonds* (see Plate IV). In a tea cosy also the weight of the design should be at the bottom and the pattern should be simple and on a small scale (see Frontispiece and Fig. 56).

To make an effective, even a rich and elaborate pattern, it is not necessary to use many different units. That may be done with good effect by an experienced designer, but a good result is more easily attained by repeating in the corners and border some of the units used in the centre, perhaps in different sizes.

Having decided on the general plan of the pattern, it is helpful to make sketches on paper. This was seldom done in the past. A girl learnt the whole art and craft of quilting so gradually: she watched her mother at work while she threaded needles for her, being allowed to put in a few stitches or mark round a template, and then worked side by side with her at the frame, thus absorbing knowledge slowly until she was able to set up, design and work a quilt alone. In these days of class teaching reinforced by study from books we must find quicker methods of learning the art of designing, and it is wise to start with simple patterns until experience brings mastery of the art.

The pattern is always marked on what will be the right side of the finished work. This material must be carefully measured and certain points marked on it, for instance the centre and the width of borders. The size of the templates needed can then be judged and they should be cut accordingly if none suitable are already to hand (see Designs and the Making of Templates). Spread the material on a big table over a thick cloth and begin to mark the pattern by placing a template in position and drawing round it with the yarn needle, which is held almost flat on the material so that it marks a line like a crease (see Fig. 62). Inside this outline the rest of the pattern is filled in by drawing with the needle in the same way. These lines will remain clear, but in case of a mistake they can be removed by damping the material and using a warm iron. Any difficult bit of pattern can be sketched provisionally with tailors' chalk, which is easily

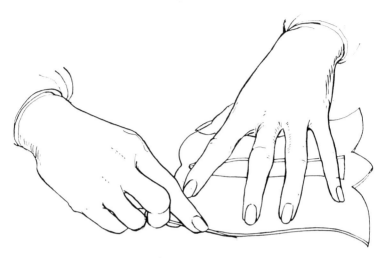

*Fig. 62. Needle-marking a template outline*

brushed off, or it can be drawn on tracing paper and needle-marked through the paper on to the material, and then needle-marked again over the faint lines. Needle-marking is recommended for final drawing because it makes a thin clean line which will not disappear. The chalk is also useful to mark guiding lines. Never use a pencil on the material.

Mark the important features of the pattern first (for instance, the centre, corners and border of a quilt) and finally put in the filling (background), choosing this with an eye to contrast; if the pattern is made up of curving lines, *basket* or *diamonds* (Figs. 49-54) form a good background, whilst *wineglass* (Figs, 4, 5) is a pleasant contrast to an angular pattern.

The *diamond* fillings which look so simple need to be marked with great care. The lines should run diagonally across the work and when interrupted by another pattern should continue along exactly the same line on the far side of it. They should all be of the same width apart and exactly parallel. If this regularity is not maintained the erratic effect will be very striking on the finished work.

Accuracy in drawing is necessary to produce a good piece of quilted work. A centre pattern should be placed exactly in the middle of the work by careful measurement; borders should keep the same width all round the work and, if they are framed by straight lines, these should be really straight. In fact, the balance of the pattern should not be thrown out by inaccurate measurement or drawing. But a certain amount of freedom in filling in the details is natural in a pattern drawn by hand and gives the pleasant effect characteristic of all good handicraft, which differentiates it from mechanical work. Thus, when filling in a feather pattern, decide how the line should swing in from the scalloped edge and grow down into the stem and, having marked the first line satisfactorily, follow its curve in marking the others. As a guide to its length note the point where it joins the stem in relation to the scallops on the opposite side. Even in a standardised pattern such as the *running feather* every worker may produce a slightly different effect by the way she fills in, and this gives her work individuality.

When the use of a few of the simple pattern units shown in this book, and a few background fillings, has been mastered, the learner will be able to plan a variety of patterns to suit any piece of quilted work. When she has acquired a wide repertory of traditional units she is ready to experiment with patterns of her own and get the same enjoyment as the quilters of the past. Remember, above all, the importance of *shapes* and that they must be simple to be effective. The leaves of many trees and plants may suggest an idea—chestnut, ivy or violet, for instance—but the natural shape should not be copied too exactly; the best quilt patterns are generally formal ones and so the shapes must be simplified and made more regular than in nature. Some quilters may find it easiest to work out a template with pencil and paper, others prefer to "worry away with the scissors". The study of quilts old and new will be productive of ideas; books with illustrations are listed in the bibliography and many museums have samples of quilted work. Sir Flinders Petrie's book contains an immense number of line drawings of patterns from antique stone carving, pottery etc., many of which can be recognised as traditional quilting units, whilst others suggest ideas for new developments. The quilter who is always on the look-out for new patterns has an abiding interest.

## Setting up the Work

When the complete pattern has been marked the work is set up in the frame. Fig. 1 shows what the frame looks like when it is put together, but first, with the frame in its four separate pieces, opposite sides of the material for the underside of the work must be sewn to the pieces of braid which are tacked to the rails. When a small piece of work is set up in a large frame it is fixed in the middle of the braid. In the case of a cushion cover or cot quilt, or something even smaller, the stretchers are now put through the slots in the rails and the four pegs fitted into holes so that the work is not stretched taut but is just loose enough to give a certain amount of play. If a big quilt is to be made some of the material must be rolled round one rail, evenly and without creases, until only about 18 in. is left; then the stretchers are fixed as described above.

Now the padding is laid on. Cotton wool or wadding should first be warmed to make it fluffy and must be handled very carefully so that the even thickness of the sheets is not displaced. For a big piece of work the sheet of cotton wool or wadding is not cut, but allowed to hang over the side of the frame. Wool must be laid on bit by bit, also being gently handled so that the staple lies in one direction, and placed to give an even thickness with no gaps. The padding should come right to the edges of the work. If a blanket is used it should be laid on and smoothed and the extra width allowed to hang over the side of the frame as in the case of wadding; its weight helps to keep it lying evenly.

The top cover, with the pattern marked on it, is next laid on to fit exactly and firmly tacked, close to the edge, along one side, the needle going through all three layers. It should be smoothed carefully over the padding but not pulled tight, and fastened along the other side with plenty of needles (or pins—see page 9). In the case of a big quilt there will of course be a lot of spare material and wadding hanging over the side, corresponding to the part of the bottom cover that is rolled round the rail; this should be rolled loosely and fastened with needles to keep it off the floor. One end of tape is now tied round a stretcher, close to the rail, "needled" to the end of the work, through all three layers, looped round the stretcher and needled to the work again 3 in. further on, and so on across the end. The other end is fastened in the same way, and thus the work will be held firmly along its four sides but not stretched or pulled out of shape. The quilter depicted in the Frontispiece is working on a fairly small quilt and as the piece left over is not long enough to touch the floor she has not found it necessary to fasten it up. The picture shows how the work should look when set up.

When a large quilt is in the frame it must be "rolled" after the piece which is set up has been stitched. The needles fastening the tapes and the far side of the work are removed; some of the unworked part is unrolled, the finished part is carefully rolled round the near rail and the work is set up again in the same way as before; it should be fixed so that the worker can comfortably continue sewing where she left off.

## Sewing the Quilt

The ends of the frame should rest steadily on two straight chair backs or trestles at a height convenient for sewing. Since the work occupies both hands the worker cannot cope with a frame which wobbles or slips. The Frontispiece shows how the quilter sits at the frame, with her left hand below the work, and that part of the quilt not yet sewn on the far side. Sewing should begin close to the rail on the near side, and this is the most difficult part. To start, without tying a knot in the cotton, insert the needle and carry it a little way through the padding; bring it up on a line of the pattern, make a backstitch and then go back over this, splitting the cotton; this holds it securely, ready to begin the running stitch, following the lines of the pattern. As each stitch is made the left hand, below, feels where the needle will come through and helps it up again, whilst the

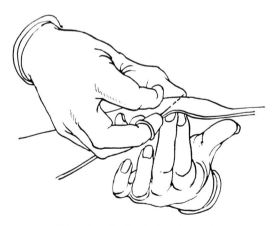

Fig. 63. Quilter's hands sewing

right thumb presses down the material just ahead of where the needle will emerge. Fig. 63 has been drawn as if the frame and work had been cut away to show the position of both hands. The quilter should not actually prick her fingers but, in case she does, a little surgical spirit used beforehand will harden the skin against damage. Take several stitches on the needle before pulling it through and try to work with a rhythmical movement, which helps to keep the stitches even. They should be the same size above and below, and the spaces should be the same length as the stitches. With a thick padding the stitches must of course be bigger, but regularity is more important than tiny stitches. Nothing looks worse than spotty little stitches with big spaces between, but very large stitches will not make the firm line needed to outline the pattern. When sewing round curves the needle must be held so that it works *away* from the user and the thumb nail is used, instead of the ball of the thumb, to help it to the surface. On a very tight curve, such as those at the edge of the *coxcomb* (Fig. 40), it may only be possible to make one stitch at a time, but generally as many stitches are taken up as can comfortably be managed. Aim ultimately at making the stitches as small as the thickness of the work allows.

When only a few inches of cotton are left in the needle, run it through the padding and bring it up, still on the line of the pattern; put it down again over only one thread of the material and repeat this until the cotton is finished. When a fresh needleful is started the new stitches will hold the end securely.

The sewing should follow a line of the pattern in its natural direction and avoid leaving short stretches to be sewn separately; for instance, in working a *rose* or a *feather*, work round a scallop and follow the line in to the centre or the stem. Work the main features of the pattern before

43

the background. Build up the pattern gradually by having several needles in action; when working diamonds, for example, instead of sewing one line as far as possible and then starting on the next, stitch a little way along one line, then carry the next one forward with another needle, then the next, and so on.

When making a big quilt it is not necessary to sew the whole of the 18-in. width which is set up in the frame; after the first rolling it will probably be convenient to work a width of only about 6 in., but there is more play in the material, making it easier to sew, if not less than 18 in. is set up.

It is possible for several quilters to work together at a large frame, all sitting on the same side; many quilts have been worked co-operatively in this way in the Women's Institutes and in the past it was often done by family groups who ran quilt clubs for a livelihood; but unless the workers have practised together until their sewing is indistinguishable the finished quilt will look very uneven.

## Finishing

When the pattern is quilted the work is taken out of the frame and the edges must be finished. The usual way is to turn them in, making sure that the padding comes to the very edge, and run a line of stitching as near to the edge as possible and a second line $\frac{1}{8}$ to $\frac{1}{4}$ in. further in (see Fig. 64). The edges should never be finished by machine stitching, which spoils the look of the work.

Piping is an alternative finish and makes a firm, neat edge. It should

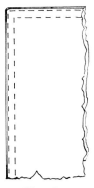

*Fig. 64.*
*Turned-in edge*

always be used for cushion covers and tea cosies, and looks well on a cot quilt. A fine piping cord should be covered in the usual way with strips of the material cut on the cross and stitched to the edge of the *under* side of the work because this, having been more tightly attached to the frame, will lie flatter than the upper side. The top cover is slip-stitched to the base of the piping (Fig. 65).

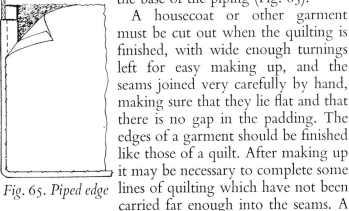

A housecoat or other garment must be cut out when the quilting is finished, with wide enough turnings left for easy making up, and the seams joined very carefully by hand, making sure that they lie flat and that there is no gap in the padding. The edges of a garment should be finished like those of a quilt. After making up it may be necessary to complete some

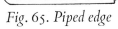

*Fig. 65. Piped edge* lines of quilting which have not been carried far enough into the seams. A quilt which has diamonds or other all-over pattern reaching to its edges, without any framed or continuous border pattern, may need to be finished in the same way; if this is neatly done it will not be noticeable.

# THE TEACHING OF QUILTING

The way in which teachers instruct their classes in quilting is of the greatest importance to the future of the craft because on this the survival of the tradition depends. The method of making a quilt and—most important of all—of planning the pattern, using the old traditional units in a new way, has hitherto been handed down in families, and the older generation of quilters still at work learnt at home in their girlhood from mother or auntie. The only way in which this ever-changing tradition and the ability, in every quilter, to design her own work, can be maintained is by the teaching of template-making and pattern-planning as part of the process of quilting. Not only will the student find it easier to learn designing in this way but also her work will be far more interesting. Pattern planning needs considerable study and practice and a wise teacher will let her students watch her during many lessons making templates and marking their shapes, while she explains how patterns are built up by the combination of simple units.

It is hard to find from the usual commercial sources good designs which are really suitable for quilting, and unsuitable ones lead to dissatisfaction when the work is finished because, however beautiful the stitching, they are not effective. Therefore a learner should never be allowed to start work on an unsatisfactory design. Similarly, she should be discouraged from copying exactly the pattern on another quilt. Traditionally "no two quilts are alike" and that is a good motto. By all means borrow templates and make drawings of pattern units, but regard these as the raw material from which new designs can be created. This book contains, in addition to a great many drawings of pattern units, a few drawings of complete patterns and some photographs of quilted work, which are included as suggestions to start the student's mind working on new variations and combinations. A list of books and patterns available will be found overleaf.

When holding a quilting class in any district an enterprising teacher will ask students to try to find old quilts and bring them to the class, where the history of the quilt, its age and place of origin should be discovered as far as possible, and the quilted patterns examined and discussed. It may be a patchwork bedcover whose quilted pattern has hardly been noticed by the owner; it may be a beautiful and treasured piece of work or rather roughly quilted; but something of interest can be found in the pattern. A visit by the class to any local museum where there are specimens of quilted work which the curator will probably, by appointment, allow students to examine closely, is another way of stimulating interest in traditional design. By such means the teacher can help students to feel that in their work they will be carrying on a valuable old tradition of handicraft of a kind whose survival in this country is now only too rare.

# BIBLIOGRAPHY

Bass, Charlotte Christiansen, *Applique Quiltmaking*, Batsford, 1984
Colby, Averil, *Quilting*, Batsford, 1983
Colby, Averil, *Patchwork Quilts*, Batsford, 1965
FitzRandolph, Mavis, *Traditional Quilting*, Batsford, 1954
Hake, Elizabeth, *English Quilting Old and New*, Batsford, 1937
Ives, Suzy, *Patterns for Patchwork Quilts and Cushions*, Batsford, 1977
Peto, Florence, *American Quilts and Coverlets*, Max Parrish and Co. Ltd, 1949
Petrie, Flinders, *Decorative Patterns of the Ancient World*, Quaritch, 1930
Short, Eirian, *Quilting: Technique, Design and Application*, Batsford, 1979
Victoria and Albert Museum, *Notes on Quilting*, H.M. Stationery Office, 1949

# PATTERNS

Some large scale drawings of pattern units and templates are obtainable from CoSIRA, 141 Castle Street, Salisbury, Wiltshire, SP1 3TP. They should be ordered by their numbers, as follows:

| | |
|---|---|
| Q3 | Borders |
| Q6 | Bell pattern—various uses |
| Q7 | Use of circle templates |
| Q9 | Border patterns |
| Q10a | Working drawing of ordinary quilt frame |
| Q10b | Working drawing of quilt frame with ratchet for turning the work |
| Q11 | Feather patterns, including border and corner feathers, square and curved feathers, feather wreath, pine feather and horse shoe |
| Q12 | Feather patterns continued, including trailing fern (Welsh), Allendale feather border, running feather (Durham) and straight feather (Northumberland) |
| Q13 | Leaf patterns, flower pot, tree used as border, fleur de lis, ivy, fern, little flourish, Welsh leaf, Welsh heart |
| Q14 | Patterns based on the circle, including rose, shell, Tudor rose, feather circle, Weardale wheel, snail creep, true lover's knot, fan |
| Q15 | Various North Country patterns : ram's horn, flat iron (Durham), scissors, goose wing, sheaf of corn, feather rose, paisley flower, banana, paisley pear (North), fleur de lis |
| Q16 | Leaves, hearts and flower patterns, flat iron (Welsh), tulip, paisley pear, heart (North), chestnut, thistle, Welsh heart |
| Q17 | Diamonds—square, double, long, Scotch, chained; basket, wineglass on diagonal and perpendicular axis, shells and fancy shells |
| Q18 | Borders : heart, worm, plait, chain, feather hammock, cord and tassel, beehives, Welsh border, tulip, tree |
| Q19 | Cable and twist variations: dog trail, Weardale chain, feather twist, trail (Welsh), lined twist, plait |
| Q20 | Bellows and star templates and strip patterns |